Career Agility

Copyright © 2021 by Veronica Millen

All rights reserved. No part of this book may be reproduced in any manner whatsoever without written permission except in the case of brief quotations embodied in critical articles and reviews.

First Printing, 2021

Career Agility

Identifying and maintaining your career sweet spot as the world of work evolves

Veronica Millen

CONTENTS

	DEDICATION	vii
1	Foreword	1
2	Introduction	3
3	Who is this book for?	5
4	How to use this book	7
5	Career agility	9
6	Skills	15
7	Interests	29
8	Needs	43
9	The job market	59
10	Bringing it all together	67
11	Bringing it to life	83
12	A note about COVID-19	89

CONTENTS

13 | Endnotes 91

14 | Thank you 97

15 | About the author 99

16 | Notes 101

"To have joy one must share it." – Lord Byron

This book is dedicated to the loves of my life: Jonathan and Eleanor. Jono and Ellie I love sharing my life with you. You make the journey, the ups and the downs, joyous. Thank you for supporting me through the journey of this book.

1

Foreword

I met Veronica on our first day as undergraduates at The University of Melbourne, before we set a foot on campus. I was eighteen, unsure about this new adventure, waiting nervously at the tram stop in front of Flinders St Station, clutching the Faculty handbook. Veronica, all of seventeen, walked up and asked me if I was heading to the University, then suggested we travel together. That was the moment a friendship was born.

That moment also typifies everything that I have both admired and envied in Veronica in the 30 years since. She has an innate interest in and desire to help others. She can see and sense what you need, connect and support you to be your best. She is a natural coach; curious, caring and collaborative.

Despite my own credentials as a coaching and workplace psychologist, Veronica has been my coach on many occasions. She has highlighted opportunities I'd have otherwise missed; asked the questions that prompt insights and always reminded me that I can.

In Career Agility you too are the recipient of Veronica's skill and care, as well as her considerable knowledge and experience of career management, developed over many years in corporate Human Resources and consulting. This book guides you through the process of discovering your career sweet spot by understanding who you are and what you need from your career. It's an insightful, practical guide grounded in psychological science and set in our current context of uncertainty and change - and Veronica is with you every step of the way, always reminding you that you can.

> Ellen Jackson
> Psychologist, Author, Podcaster
> Potential Psychology

Ellen is a psychologist, internationally published author, speaker and consultant to organisations Australia-wide. Ellen's passion is helping people and their workplaces to understand the ins and out of human behaviour and to use this knowledge to achieve their goals. Everything she teaches is supported by scientific research, so she knows it works. She overlays this with a nuanced understanding of individuals and how they function to help you and your workplace to thrive and flourish. She loves what she does, and her greatest joy is seeing others implement the simple, effective strategies that she teaches to thrive and flourish. Ellen runs a business called Potential Psychology https://www.potential.com.au/ and also has an amazing podcast series that I highly recommend, also called Potential Psychology, that was a finalist in the 2019 Australian Podcast Awards.

2

Introduction

I love my work. I love coaching people and supporting them to be their best and to love their work too. That is why I am writing this book: to help as many people as possible to find work they enjoy and continue to enjoy as the world of work changes and evolves.

For more than 25 years I have worked in Human Resources, mostly in large corporations but also in consulting firms. I coach people one on one and consult to companies of various sizes across many industries including banking, retail and property, to name a few.

One thing that has struck me over this time is how many people are unhappy in their day-to-day jobs or longer-term careers. Many don't do anything about it because they don't invest the time or don't know what they want to do, or both. Others are reasonably happy but don't feel an overwhelming alignment or sense of purpose in their work. Many people I have spoken to, whether it be colleagues, clients, friends or family, don't know how to work out what they want to do, or feel it's all too hard. This amazes me – that we spend so much time at work and often do so little to ensure we are happy there. I know sometimes I have spent more time planning a holiday or renovation than I have on actively managing my career!

More and more these days, companies are restructuring, so even if we have been happy in our jobs, our roles may be made redundant due to cost cutting or automation. Also, as we get older, often our life circumstances change. For example, we might have a family and value flexibility more highly than we did when we first started working.

While no job will be perfect, I believe we can all find jobs in the short term and careers in the longer term that are well suited to us and which we enjoy. That is the purpose of this book: to give you the tools to determine what kind of work you would like and be good at, which aligns with your values, and is needed in the job market. In sum, to help you find your career sweet spot.

This practical workbook outlines a 'career agility' model, then walks you through the model step by step. As each part of the model is explained, I include exercises, tools, templates and examples to support you in applying the model to your personal circumstances. I encourage you to complete the exercises as you read the book to get the most out of the process. You might like to use the blank templates provided or a separate notebook – whatever works for you.

This book is not about landing your dream job. There are lots of how-to tools out there to help you write your resume, prepare for a job interview or write a great LinkedIn profile. This book is about working out what your dream job or career sweet spot is and remaining agile so you can keep it, even as the world of work changes and evolves around you.

3

Who is this book for?

You may:

- be reasonably happy in your work but feel it could be better aligned to your personal values and interests;
- feel you want to make some changes before you become increasingly dissatisfied with your work and career;
- have let things get to the point where you are desperately unhappy but don't know what you would rather be doing;
- have just finished school or university, and be unsure what you want to do next, or have a child who is in that position and want to support them;
- be a career coach with great skills in terms of resume writing, developing LinkedIn profiles and interview preparation, but want to build your toolkit to support your clients find greater job and career satisfaction through identifying their purpose;
- be working in Human Resources within a large organisation that restructures regularly and want to be able to support employees and people leaders with some practical career management tools; or
- have been made redundant or taken parental leave and are at a career crossroads, wanting to take some time to reflect and evaluate what to do next.

Whatever your personal circumstances, this book is for you if you want some practical guidance and are willing to put some time and effort into doing the exercises provided to help you find and maintain your career sweet spot.

While everyone's sweet spot will be different based on their individual skills, interests and values, the process we use to discover each person's career sweet spot is the same.

4

How to use this book

This book is like your own personal career coach giving you all the tools you need to find your career sweet spot, guiding you through the process step by step.

The first focus is on skills, then interests, needs, and the job market; and then on bringing it all together. Some real-life examples help bring the model to life, and I have also included a note about the COVID-19 pandemic given its big impact on the world of work.

There is no right or wrong way to approach the exercises or answer the questions that follow. The examples provided are deliberately included after the exercises and questions because you may have enough ideas to start reflecting and writing; and if that is the case I don't want the example to restrict your thinking. If you don't quite understand what the exercise is asking of you, or no thoughts come to mind, you can read the examples and use them as thought starters.

I encourage you to take the time you need to complete each exercise and think deeply about your answers. I have found that people who do so have gained far greater value from the exercises. You may need to go away and reflect and then come back and document your thoughts. You might want to talk to people who know you well about your reflections.

Some exercises may be more relevant than others. Invest time in the exercises that are pertinent to you and limit the time (or possibly even skip) any exercises you find less relevant, although I suggest you complete at least one exercise in each of the key elements (skills, interests, needs).

Like most things in life, the results you get are correlated with the effort you put in.

So, let's go!

5

Career agility

What is career agility?

You may have heard of the project management methodology 'agile', which is used in many large corporations. Some of you, like me, may have worked in agile workplaces with regular 'stand ups', 'Kanban walls' and 'retrospectives'. Others may be wondering what agile is and how it applies to their career.

Agile management grew out of the software development industry.[1] The high-level principles of agile management are:

- the law of the small team;
- the law of the customer; and
- the law of the network.[2]

The concept of career agility is not strictly based on these principles but rather the overarching agile management idea of 'survival through flexibility'.[3]

With the changing nature of the global workplace, it is increasingly important for you to be able to identify the skills, jobs and career trends that are valued in the market and adapt accordingly. While you are adapting, you want to ensure you remain aligned with your personal attributes, for example your interests and values.

The process and practical tools in this book will build your career agility – a skill that you can use throughout your life and career.

Once you have read this book and applied what you have learned, you may choose to revisit some or all of the exercises in years to come as you grow, and the world of work evolves.

The career agility model

I know this model works as I have seen it in action firsthand. I have used this model with lots of clients and in many organisations. I have seen people apply the model with great success. Therefore, I am confident that this model will help you.

You may have friends or know people who seemingly have a 'dream job' or 'dream career'. They may have landed there through hard work or luck, but they cannot always articulate the 'formula' or process they followed to get there. I believe they probably followed the formula or model I outline in this book but may have done so intuitively and that's why they can't always articulate the steps and process to you.

Many inspirational and quote books tell us to follow our dreams or do what we love. These phrases are great but a little too simplistic and don't provide the tools and guidance many of us need.

The career agility model is based on a Venn diagram that is used by many career coaches and outplacement/career transition organisations in varying forms, but with the same underlying premise. The Venn diagram on the next page shows your career sweet spot as the intersection of:

- your skills
- your interests
- your needs/values.

In the following chapters, I will bring each of these areas to life for you, providing practical ways of exploring them in as much – or as little – depth as you would like. Then I will help you bring it all together. My aim is that by the end of this book you will have identified what you want to do and what your dream job/career sweet spot is – or at least be closer to it than when you started reading.

The origins of the career agility model

The origin of this approach to finding your ideal job/career sweet spot is not known.

It is possibly derived from the Japanese concept of *Ikigai*. According to the Japanese, everyone has an *Ikigai*, which is essentially a reason to get up in the morning, a reason for being. Your *Ikigai* lies at the centre of the interconnecting circles illustrated in the diagram below.[4]

The career agility approach is more streamlined but along the same lines.

Once you understand what you are good at (your skills), what you enjoy doing (your interests) and what you need (your personal work values), you can then bring this together to identify your career sweet spot.

VERONICA MILLEN

6

Skills

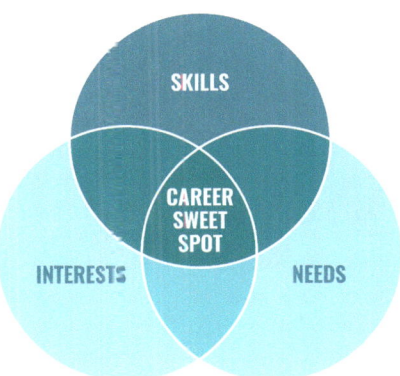

Your skills are important as they mean you have the ability to get the job done. If you find a career or job that aligns with your interests and values, but you don't have the skills, you will then need to ask yourself whether you are willing to gain the skills required. This may mean undertaking further studies and/or work experience.

It is vitally important that you have the skills and abilities, or capacity to gain the skills, required for a role if you are to be employable and if you are to enjoy it.

Think about your skills broadly, not just those you have been trained in through education or developed in the workplace, but skills you have acquired in your life through your involvement in sports clubs or volunteering, for example, or through a hobby.

Identify your skills - the following exercises will support you to identify your skills

Exercise one

Spend some time thinking about your skills and write a list. For this exercise, no idea is a bad idea or wrong, simply brainstorm all the things you are good at both at work and at home, or as some corporates now call it, have an 'ideas rave'.

Write all your thoughts here or in your notebook:

_____
_____
_____
_____
_____
_____
_____
_____
_____
_____

For example:

I believe some of my skills are:

- project management;
- time management;
- negotiation;
- relationship building;
- stakeholder **management**; and
- some technical Human Resources skills.

Exercise two

Review the following list of skills and identify those that apply to you and write them in the space available in this book or in your notebook:

Leadership and management skills:

- Advising
- Coaching
- Conflict resolution
- Decision making
- Delegating
- Diplomacy
- Interviewing
- Motivating
- Problem solving
- Strategic thinking

Organisational skills:

- Categorising data
- Co-ordinating
- Goal setting
- Meeting deadlines
- Multi-tasking
- Prioritising
- Project management
- Scheduling
- Strategic planning
- Time management

Team building skills:

- Collaboration
- Communication
- Flexibility
- Listening
- Observation
- Participation
- Respect
- Sharing

Analytical skills

- Critical thinking
- Data analysis
- Numeracy
- Reporting
- Research
- Troubleshooting

Skills list adapted from Yourdictionary.com, Love To Know, 2020.

_____
_____
_____
_____
_____
_____
_____
_____
_____

Exercise three

What skills have you gained from your previous roles? Spend some time thinking about this and write your answers in the table below or in your notebook. You may like to think about non-paid roles, for example sporting committees and volunteer work, as well as the paid jobs you have had.

As much as possible, try and think about your skills in the broadest possible sense, so that rather than expressing a skill relative to the job you were in when you developed and used the skill, write it down as a more general skill. This will help later in the process when you are bringing your skills, interests and needs together, as you will be able to consider the skills that can be transferred if required.

Previous roles	Skills

For example:

Previous roles	Skills
Remuneration Analyst	• Analysing the size of a job using Hay job evaluation methodology. The size of the job helps determine the appropriate remuneration range in conjunction with the job market. (Note: I could have captured this as 'Hay job evaluation', but I have tried to make this a little broader, which will help me later when I come to think about transferrable skills.) • Numeracy • Excel
Workforce Planning Analyst	• Project management • Analysis
Human Resource Business Partner	• Problem-solving • Influencing • Stakeholder management

Exercise four

What feedback have you received about your skills? Think about skills you may not have realised you have until others mentioned them. For example, I remember one woman I coached telling me how she was often praised for being able to manage a budget, but thought to herself 'doesn't everyone do that?' I helped her realise that not everyone can do that and managing a budget was a key skill that she possessed.

I encourage you to spend some time thinking about feedback (past and current), performance appraisals and position descriptions to help you identify some of your work skills and then write down your thoughts in the space provided in this book or in your notebook.

_____
_____
_____
_____
_____
_____
_____
_____
_____
_____

For example:

In many of my past performance review meetings, my managers have praised me for always meeting my deadlines. While I thought that was what was expected and common practice, on reflection, perhaps I do have strong skills in time management and delivering on time.

Assess your level of skill proficiency

Exercise five

Take some time to assess your current level of proficiency for all of your skills or at least your top/key skills.

You may choose to conduct a self-assessment. You may also ask others for feedback and then compare your analysis with the feedback you receive.

Your current level of proficiency for your key skills will become important in the future when you are moving to the stage of trying to land a job in your career sweet spot. I would encourage you then to assess the skill level required for the job and your current skill level and if there is a difference, determine a plan of action to close the gap. You need to be honest with yourself about whether you are willing to take the action that is required to close any gaps, particularly if you have any large skill gaps.

You may like to use the table below to assess your current level of skill proficiency or write in your notebook.

Skill	Proficiency level		
	Basic	Intermediate	Advanced

For example:

Skill	Proficiency level		
	Basic	Intermediate	Advanced
Excel	X		
Project management	X		
Stakeholder management		X	

Consider your transferrable skills

Exercise six

Think about your skills from a transferability point of view. This is one of the reasons I asked you earlier to think about skills in a broad sense.

Spend some time now thinking about your skills, even skills that are specific to a particular job or company or training course, and think about how they could be transferred to another job or company or industry.

List below or in your notebook your first brain dump of all your transferrable skills:

For example:

Skill

Analysis and decision-making. As outlined earlier, I have skills in analysing the size of a job using Hay job evaluation methodology. Gaining and using accreditation in Hay job evaluation enabled me to build strong analytical and decision-making skills that I could apply in other work contexts.

Chairing a meeting. I have chaired lots of Human Resources (HR) meetings and am confident I could chair meetings for other professions as I have the skills to ensure that we are keeping to the timings on the agenda etc.

Taking minutes. Again, I have taken minutes for lots of HR meetings and am confident I would be able to take minutes for meetings for other professions.

MS Office i.e. proficient in Word, Excel and PowerPoint. I have used the MS Office suite of products extensively in my HR career and am confident that these skills are transferrable to other professions.

Exercise seven

Now spend some time considering whether you can reframe your thinking about some of the other skills you have developed over your life. This deeper analysis may help you realise that some of your skills re-named and considered from another angle could also be transferrable. You can review your answers from previous exercises and also see if you can come up with any new thoughts.

In the table that follows or in your notebook list any other skills you have now identified as transferrable:

Skill	Reframed skill so it is transferrable

For example:

Skill	Reframed skill so it is transferrable
Remuneration analyst – hay job evaluation accreditation (from exercise three)	Critical thinking and/or decision-making
Chairing the diversity committee (from exercise six i.e chairing a meeting)	Running meetings
Accredited to run Myers–Briggs Type Indicator workshops (new thought)	Workshop facilitation

Your top five skills

Reviewing all your answers to the questions about skills (exercises 1 to 7), what are your top three to five work skills? Spend some time thinking about this and write down your answers below or in your notebook.

1. _____

2. _____

3. _____

4. _____

5. _____

7

Interests

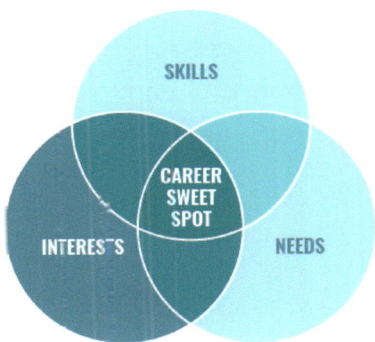

Your interests are your preferences, the things you enjoy doing.

Your interests are important to ensure you are enjoying your time at work. Research shows that on average we spend one third of our life at work.[5] You don't want to be spending your time on things that you are good at if you don't like them.

One client I coached was good at arranging events because she worried about everything that could go wrong and planned to ensure that it wouldn't. Her worrying and planning ensured that her events went well but she didn't enjoy the event planning aspect of her work. People were always saying to her that the events she planned were so good and that therefore she should go into full-time event management. What they didn't realise was that while she was good at organising events, she didn't particularly enjoy it.

From this you can see that while we are initially looking at each element of the model independently, it is important later in the book that I bring all of the elements together for you to determine your career sweet spot, because each element is inter-connected. For you to truly be in your sweet spot, a job needs to meet all three elements: your skills, your interests and your needs.

Let's move on now to how you can identify what your interests or preferences are.

Identify your interests - the following exercises will support you to identify your interests

Exercise eight

What do you like doing from a work context? Start by spending some time thinking about this and write a list. For this exercise, no idea is a bad idea, simply brainstorm all the things you like to do at work and write them down below or in your notebook.

_____
_____
_____
_____
_____
_____
_____
_____

For example:

- I like working with people.
- I like being part of a team.
- I like being considered a subject-matter expert.
- I like being able to see the tangible results of my actions.

Exercise nine

What do you like doing outside of work, i.e. your hobbies, interests, volunteering, spare time? Spend some time thinking about this and write a list. Again, for this exercise no idea is a bad idea, simply brainstorm all the things you like to do and write them down below or in your notebook.

_____
_____
_____
_____
_____
_____
_____

For example:

- I love photography.
- I like shopping.
- I like dancing.

Exercise ten

Now think about whether any of the above non-work-related interests can be used in a work context. Write your reflections below or in your notebook.

_____
_____
_____
_____
_____
_____
_____

For example:

- Photography – creativity, how can I include some level of creativity into my work?
- Shopping – possibly working in retail? Possibly consumer research?
- Dancing – energy and fun in the workplace?

A friend of mine loves listening to music. She works for an opera company in the corporate office. She loves working in the music industry and working for a company whose purpose aligns with one of her core interests. Not all of us are able to achieve this alignment, but hopefully this gives you some food for thought.

For any interests that can't be met in a work context, I would encourage you to see how they can be incorporated into other aspects of your life.

Someone I was coaching in the past loved singing and while she wasn't able to do this at her work, she did join a choir and found that singing in her local choir fortnightly was thoroughly enjoyable and met her musical interest or preference. She was able to incorporate some of her other interests into her profession.

Exercise eleven

What did you like doing as a child? Spend some time now thinking about the things you loved doing when you were young. Remember back to the games you liked to play and the toys you liked to play with. Did you love to draw, run or play imaginary games? Try and remove current practicalities and reality from your mind and think back to your childhood years and the things you were drawn to, and the activities you really enjoyed before you had responsibilities and to-do lists. Write down your memories and thoughts from this reflection below or in your notebook.

_____
_____
_____
_____
_____
_____
_____

For example:

When I was a child and we had friends over, I used to love playing schools and always wanted to be the teacher. I would draw up a timetable and organise what we were going to do and when. I would ask my younger sister and her friends to be the students. I would give each 'student' a basket filled with notebooks and stationery and then ask them to sit behind the basket and pretend it was their school desk. Now, as an adult, I really enjoy facilitating workshops and wonder if this is perhaps linked to the enjoyment I got as a child from playing schools and pretending to be the teacher.

Exercise twelve

Review your previous job roles, then spend some time thinking about what you liked about these roles. What part of the job did you most enjoy? What gave you energy? Some people call this type of exercise an 'archaeological dig'; others might call this appreciative enquiry. Document your answers in the table below or in your notebook.

Some of my previous clients have also spoken to their family members/partners/housemates who have said things like 'remember you used to always come home and complain about "x"' or 'you used to always enjoy "y" about that job', which helped to trigger their memory.

Also, if there are any elements in a role that you really want to make sure you avoid in the future, note these in the table below or in your notebook as well.

Previous roles	Interests/Preferences	Things to avoid

For example:

Previous roles	Interests/Preferences	Things to avoid
Remuneration analyst	Learning from the remuneration managers – love of learning (also feeds into my love of being a subject-matter expert)	Data/numbers are not things that come naturally to me nor do I find complex mathematics easy or fun. I found this out when studying maths for economics at university and it has been confirmed many times at work since.
Diversity manager	Stakeholder relations/ stakeholder management	Data and reporting – I didn't enjoy this nor was I particularly good at this.

Or, if you prefer, you could graph your career to date as per this example.[6]

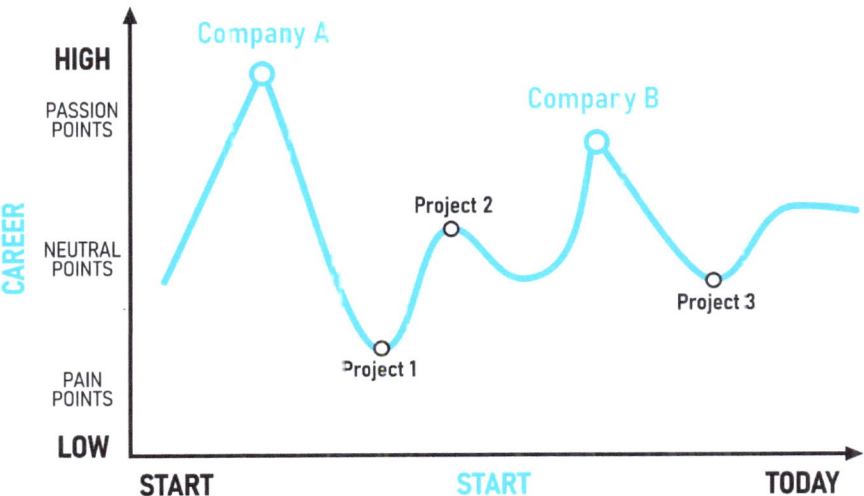

Here is a blank template for you to use if you would like to take this approach:

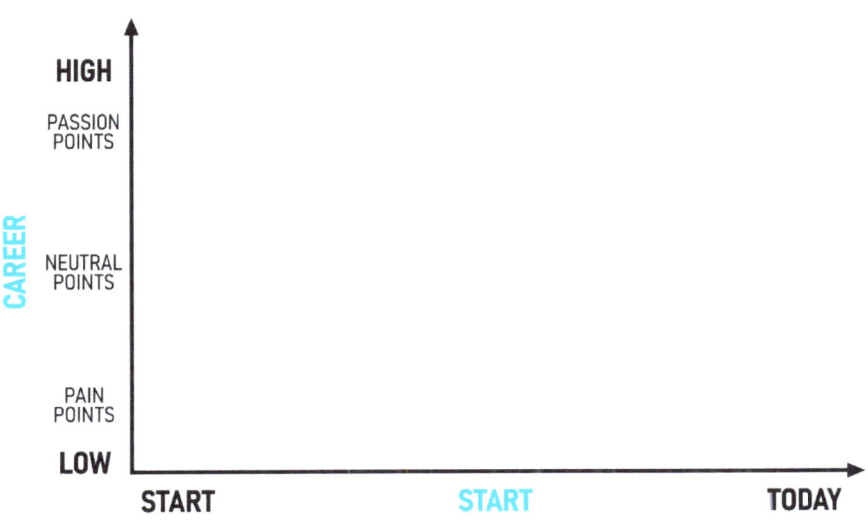

Exercise thirteen

You may have heard of the concept of 'flow'. If not, you might like to watch Mihaly Csikszentmihalyi's TED Talk 'Flow, the secret to happiness',[7] which has been viewed more than 5 million times.

Flow can be described as those moments when you are completely absorbed in a challenging but doable task. I think of flow of when I lose track of time as I am so focused and enjoying what I am doing that everything else fades away.

Mihaly Csikszentmihalyi, considered one of the co-founders of positive psychology, was the first to identify and research flow. The experience of flow is universal and has been reported to occur across all classes, genders, ages and cultures, and it can be experienced during many types of activities.

If you've ever heard someone describe a time when their performance excelled and they were 'in the zone', they were likely describing an experience of flow. Flow occurs when your skill level and the challenge at hand are equal.

Csikszentmihalyi describes eight characteristics of flow:

1. complete concentration on the task;
2. clarity of goals and reward in mind and immediate feedback;
3. transformation of time (speeding up/slowing down);
4. the experience is intrinsically rewarding;
5. effortlessness and ease;
6. there is a balance between challenge and skills;
7. actions and awareness are merged, losing self-conscious rumination;
8. there is a feeling of control over the task.[8]

Take some time now to reflect and think about whether you have ever been in flow, whether at work or outside of work. Have you ever been completely focused on a task and lost track of time? Read the eight characteristics above and think about whether you have ever been in a situation where all of those characteristics have applied, and you were in flow. Write down below or in your note book your thoughts and reflections about whether you have been in flow in the past and whether this provides you with any insights into your work preferences.

_____
_____
_____
_____
_____
_____
_____
_____

For example:

I love photography and I recall many years ago hiring a dark room in a local library with a friend from work. We would hire the darkroom for a few hours and process our film and black-and-white photos. I really loved watching the photo images almost emerge onto the paper. I remember when the employees from the library would knock on the door to tell us our time would be up in ten minutes. We were both shocked at how quickly the time had gone – we were in the zone. We were both so focused and we had lost track of time as we concentrated at the task on hand. I had to really think about how much of each chemical was required and how to use the projector. I enjoyed it and was challenged by it; I believe I was in flow.

Exercise fourteen

Write below or in your notebook what you would like to do if you had the day off tomorrow and didn't have to worry about chores or bills or family responsibilities. Again, like in any brainstorm session, no idea is right or wrong.

_____
_____
_____
_____
_____
_____
_____

For example:

If I had the day off tomorrow, some of the things I would like to do include:

- shopping – I have worked in retail (both on the shop floor and in corporate head offices) and really enjoyed the industry;
- catching up with friends – I am extroverted and love working with people. While I like some time by myself, I don't enjoy long periods alone (at home or at work);
- organising my house – I like some degree of structure to my work and I have also considered becoming a personal organiser. I love renovating and decorating my own home and watching home improvement shows. I also enjoy going to open for inspections and auctions. I have worked in the property industry and while it was in the Human Resources team, I really enjoyed being part of the industry and would be happy to work in it again.

A more in-depth look at interests

If you want to take an even more in-depth look at interests and preferences, many career coaches – including me! – are accredited in tools such as the Myers–Briggs Type Indicator (MBTI) or the Birkman Method. A coach can work with you face to face or remotely using online communication platforms such as Zoom to support you in a more detailed analysis of your preferences and interests using a scientifically valid and reliable tool.

Please note, some of the free tools online are good and others should be avoided as they are not scientifically valid and reliable. Also, free online tools don't include a debrief from someone accredited in the tool who can explain what the tool's terminology means, help you understand and interpret your results, or answer any questions you may have.

Your top five interests

Looking at all of your answers to the questions about interests (exercises 8 to 14), what are your top three to five work interests? You may need to invest considerable time thinking about this over a period of time. Once you have some clarity, write down your answers below or in your notebook.

1. _____

2. _____

3. _____

4. _____

5. _____

8

Needs

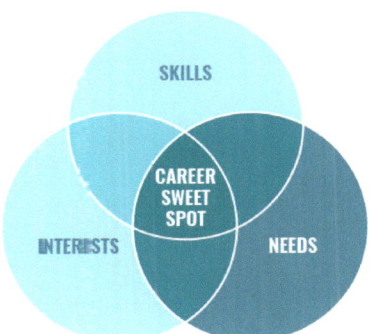

Needs are the third and final element to consider when determining your career sweet spot.

Your needs can also be defined as your work values. It is important that your work needs are met for you to feel satisfied and fulfilled at work. When your work does not align with your personal work values, it will be hard to sustain this situation for long periods of time.

Individuals will have different underlying needs or work values, and these may change over time as your personal circumstances change. For example, when I started my career, I valued career advancement and working in the city. I was single and had just graduated from university and was keen to progress and work close to friends so I could catch up with them for lunch or drinks after work. Now I have a family and career progression is not a need for me. I value work-life balance and prefer to work closer to home. This may change as my daughter grows up, but at the moment my needs or work values are clear and different to when I began working. Being clear on your needs means you can ensure that your work aligns with those needs.

Identify your needs - the following exercises will support you to identify your needs

Exercise fifteen

I recommend that you take the time to really think about what you value and need from your work. Take some time to brainstorm your needs or work values and document them below. As I have said for each brainstorm, no idea is good or bad, just write down everything that comes to mind below or in your notebook.

_____
_____
_____
_____
_____
_____

For example - I need and value the following:

- flexibility – the ability to start late sometimes to take my daughter to school, for instance;
- interesting work – work that I find challenging and enjoyable;
- ongoing learning – I love learning new things and applying new skills;
- a good culture – it is really important to me that the culture of the company I am working for is positive;
- alignment with a company's purpose – I need to feel as though my personal values are well aligned with the organisation's values;
- a good team – I enjoy a positive team environment where my teammates and I get along and work well together. I love collaborating with my colleagues and learning from each other;
- work that is close to home – I am happy when my commute is short.

At the start of exercise sixteen, I ask you to brainstorm your values before I provide a list. I did this deliberately as sometimes once we have seen a list it can be difficult for any of us to think about anything other than what is on the list. Now that you have completed your brainstorm, I will provide a list of work values for you to review.

Rank your needs

Exercise sixteen

Your values can be grouped into different categories or types. One way of grouping values is into the following classifications: intrinsic values, extrinsic values and lifestyle values.

Intrinsic values or motivation are things that we are intrinsically or internally motivated to value. Extrinsic values are things that we value that are external to us. Daniel Bortz has provided a good list of values using these two categories and some other groupings (see below).[9] Daniel recommends that people rank how important these values are to them on a scale of 1 to 5, with 5 being the most important and 1 being the least important, and I really like this approach.

Spend some time now reviewing the list and rating the values. Once you have rated all of the values listed, look at the values you rated 5 as these are your top work values. While the others are still important, the fives are probably your 'deal breakers'. If you have lots of fives (e.g. ten or more) I recommend you review your list and try and scale if down to five or six as it may be difficult to find a job that meets all of your priorities – your list in this instance may be aspirational and not all that realistic.

Intrinsic values:

- having variety and change at work
- helping others
- feeling respected at work
- taking risks
- having your work recognised.

Extrinsic values:

- travelling for work
- collecting a big pay cheque
- setting your own hours
- having time off work
- having autonomy at work.

Lifestyle values:

- spending time with friends and family
- living in a big city
- living abroad
- saving money
- becoming a homeowner.

For example: I completed the exercise for my own personal value set:

Intrinsic values	My ranking
Having variety and change at work	4
Helping others	4
Feeling respected at work	5
Taking risks	1
Having your work recognised	4
Extrinsic values	
Travelling for work	1
Collecting a big pay cheque	3
Setting your own hours	5
Having time off work	3
Having autonomy at work	5
Lifestyle values	
Spending time with friends and family	4
Living in a big city	3
Living abroad	1
Saving money	4
Becoming a homeowner	4

By completing this, I can see that being respected, setting my own hours (to spend time with my family) and having autonomy are my top work values. This aligns well with my reflections from other exercises I have completed.

Exercise seventeen

You may also like to undertake a work values identification exercise such as CareerPerfect's InSight Values Work Characteristics Inventory or 123test's Work Values Test. Both are free online tools and can be accessed via my website at **www.veronicamillen.com/career-agility**.

Once you have completed one or both of these online tools, document below or in your notebook any insights and key work values you determined from completing these exercises.

_____
_____
_____
_____
_____
_____

For example:

I completed the 123test Work Values Test and 'work-life balance' is an area where I scored above average compared to the reference group. This doesn't surprise me given my desire to balance spending time with my primary-school-aged daughter and work.

Similarly, when I completed the CareerPerfect work values questionnaire, time autonomy and work location came up in my 'high-valued' category, which rings true for me at this stage of my life in terms of what I value professionally.

Identify the role of work in your life

Exercise eighteen

Work is important not just for financial reasons. Work can play an important role in our lives for many other reasons including providing social connection, a sense of purpose, meaningful use of time and mental functionality.

Richard P. Johnson (former president of the American Association for Adult Development and Aging, and founder of the Retirement Options consultancy for mature life planning) says that these are the five benefits (perhaps even needs) that collectively bring us satisfaction through our work:

- financial remuneration
- time management
- socialisation
- status/identity
- utility/usefulness.[19]

According to evidence from the *World Happiness Report*, published annually to coincide with the United Nations' International Day of Happiness:

"Being unemployed is miserable. One of the most robust findings in the economics of happiness is that unemployment is destructive to people's wellbeing. We find this is true around the world. The employed evaluate the quality of their lives much more highly on average as compared to the unemployed. Individuals who are unemployed also report around 30 percent more negative emotional experiences in their day-to-day lives. The importance of having a job extends far beyond the salary attached to it. A large stream of research has shown that the non-monetary aspects of

employment are also key drivers of people's wellbeing. Social status, social relations, daily structure, and goals all exert a strong influence on people's happiness."[11]

Take some time to really think about the role of work in your life. What role does it play for you? Consider this in terms of the five functions of work outlined previously (financial remuneration; time management; socialisation; status/identity; and utility/usefulness). Write down below or in your notebook what you think you need from work.

_____
_____
_____
_____
_____
_____
_____

For example:

There was a time when I would daydream about winning the lottery and never working again. I thought that if I didn't have to work, I would be happy. Down the track, I took a redundancy and had a break before looking for my next role. What I found out in that time is that not working is not for me. I need and want purpose, structure and social interaction. Without these I can feel a little lonely, lost and unproductive. This was a big revelation for me, as I had underestimated how much work fulfils these needs until I didn't work for a while. While I kept busy and did some consulting work, I found that wasn't enough for my personal individual needs. This was such a great learning for me and helped shape what I look for in a role. I now know I value:

- working with others;
- structure;
- being part of a team;
- a feeling of purpose; and
- feeling like my work is adding value.

While these are my preferences and values, it's important to note I respect and admire people who choose unpaid or voluntary work. For example, one of my best friends is a 'stay-at-home mum' to three beautiful children. She helps at the local school library, plans exciting family road trips and does amazing things with and for her extended family. She works really hard and gets a lot out of what she does even though she is not remunerated financially for it. She finds it fulfilling in many other ways. And so, the methodology in this book equally applies to people who work in unpaid ways, such as stay-at-home mums or dads, volunteers and retirees.

Exercise nineteen

Now it's time for another 'archaeological dig'. Think back through your working life and consider any particular highs or lows through your 'values' lens. Really take your time to think about your personal values and how they aligned – or didn't align – to the values of the company you worked for; not just their espoused values (the ones on the posters etc.) but those in use daily in the workplace. Were there any times in the past that you felt particularly aligned or unaligned? Detail below or in your notebook any reflections you have and any important values this exercise surfaces for you.

_____
_____
_____
_____
_____

For example:

I took a job in a gaming and entertainment company many years ago. It was interesting work, and the people were lovely, but my values didn't align to the values of the organisation. I didn't feel comfortable doing tours of the casinos and seeing people standing at the slot machines who appeared to have a gambling addiction – and who possibly couldn't afford to be spending more – putting coins in, and thinking 'this is where my income comes from'. This is not a value judgement of others who work in that industry, it just made me realise it didn't fit for me. I had thought I wouldn't mind where I worked (within reason), but this experience made me realise that values alignment was important to me. It doesn't just need to be alignment in terms of the overall purpose of the company, it can also be the way the company does business and how the values are lived by the employees, particularly by the leaders who set the tone.

A note about purpose

Some of you may be wondering how purpose (life purpose and or career purpose) fits with the career agility model.

For anyone interested in doing more work on uncovering their life purpose, I highly recommend the book *Find Your Why* by Simon Sinek, David Mead and Peter Docker, published in 2017. In their book they write:

> *"Every one of us has a WHY, a deep-seated purpose, cause or belief that is the source of our passion and inspiration ... Happiness comes from what we do. Fulfillment comes from why we do it ... Once you know your WHY, you have a choice to live it every day."*[12]

(I reveal my 'why' in the introduction to this book!)

The authors go on to outline a process for discovering your why. In sum, it involves three keep steps:

1. Gather stories and share them.
2. Identify themes.
3. Draft and refine a 'why' statement.

The authors note that "there is no shortcut to discovering your WHY. Think of it as working out. The more time you put into it, the more you get out of it".[13]

Career Agility is focused on helping you to find and keep your career sweet spot as the world of work evolves. While this is different to finding your purpose, there are some obvious connections – for example, if your work is aligned with your purpose, you are far more likely to have career fulfilment.

While your life purpose can be far broader than work in terms of the career agility model, I include career or life purpose in the needs segment (covered in this chapter). If you have spent time uncovering your purpose, it can be important for your work to align with your purpose for you to be fulfilled and therefore to be in your career sweet spot.

Australian work reinvention expert, Joanne Maxwell, writes in her great book *Rethink your career in your 40s, 50s and 60s*, "Passion is not the same as purpose, but they are connected. If passion is 'I love my work', then purpose is 'I have a strong sense of direction and meaning, and I feel life is worth living'."[14] Using the career agility model, your passions are covered in the interests segment (see Chapter 7).

There are some other professionals who do great work in terms of purpose and whose work I really admire, including Megan Dalla-Camina[15] and Lorraine Murphy.[16] I found Lorraine's podcast entitled 'How To Connect With Your Purpose" particularly insightful (episode 85, 26 March 2021). If you are interested in delving into finding your purpose more deeply, I highly recommend looking them up. Jack Delosa[17] is also a great person to follow on Instagram in relation to personal development and purpose.

Exercise twenty

If you have a clear sense of your career and or life purpose, then please write down below or in your notebook your thoughts about your purpose and how it relates to your needs for work.

_____
_____
_____
_____
_____
_____
_____

For example:

My career purpose is to educate and coach people so that they can be their best – particularly in their professional lives – whether they are a first-time people leader or someone at a career crossroads. In sum, it's to bring out the best in people. This is something I love and am passionate about. It is also something I believe I have some natural interest and am talented in. I have formal training and qualifications as a coach. My coaching work fits well with my lifestyle needs and personal values. It ticks all the boxes for me. While there are some hard days and parts of the job I don't love (the administration side of it), overall, my work aligns well with my career purpose and the other elements of the career agility model.

Your top five work needs

Unfortunately, it is unlikely that one job will have everything you desire or need. Sometimes in life we need to make trade-offs. We need to decide what are non-negotiable needs that we must have met and what are desires or things that we would like to have or that would be nice to have.

Looking at all the work values exercises you have completed (exercises 15 to 19), take some time now to think about what your top three to five work needs are and write down your answers below or in your notebook.

1. _____

2. _____

3. _____

4. _____

5. _____

9

The job market

So far, the exercises in this book have asked you to look at yourself – your skills, your interests, and your needs. These are all important. As Socrates is credited with saying, the unexamined life is not worth living. It is also important to examine our environment, in this case the job market.

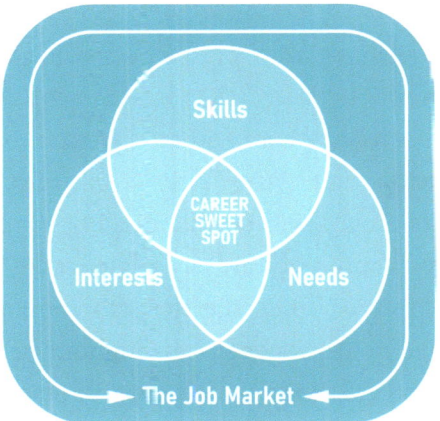

The job market is vital because unless we are independently wealthy and can afford to work as a volunteer, it is no good finding work that you have the skills for, enjoy and meets your personal needs/values if it is unpaid, doesn't pay enough to pay your bills, or is on its way to being redundant due to technological changes, for example.

The job market is rapidly changing, and a lot has been written about the 'fourth revolution' and the future of work. Now that you have completed your internal reflection, I encourage you to look to the external job market and start to research.

Through researching and learning about the job market you may find jobs emerging that haven't previously existed and that align with your skills, interests and needs. For example I have done a lot of work in the Diversity and Inclusion (D&I) area and yet D&I roles didn't exist when I started working in HR. If I had been fixed on doing one type of work for all of my career I could have missed out on moving into this interesting and rewarding area.

Having built my D&I skills and experience on the job also helped when my broader HR role was made redundant as part of a corporate restructure; because I was able to find another job quickly in the more specialised D&I space as it was a growing part of the job market.

I am sure that when my now primary-school-aged daughter enters the workforce there will be many jobs for her to consider that currently don't exist. When I was at school and talking to my careers counsellor jobs like App Developer and You Tuber didn't exist and the speed of change is only increasing. I will be encouraging my daughter to focus on her skills, interests and needs as they relate to the job market rather than one specific job type when she starts to contemplate her career. I will also encourage her to stay agile throughout her career so that as her skills/interests/needs change and as the job market evolves she can adjust accordingly.

One report states "the number of jobs you may have in your lifetime will likely be double that of a generation ago"[18] and another states "it's more likely that a 15-year-old today will experience a portfolio career, potentially having 17 different jobs over five careers in their lifetime". [19]

The growth of artificial intelligence and the gig economy

According to global business advisory firm Deloitte, the future of work is shaped by two powerful forces: the growing adoption of artificial intelligence (AI) in the workplace, and the expansion of the workforce to include both on- and off-balance-sheet talent.[20]

While artificial intelligence can sound scary, all the research I have done says that AI will augment and work with humans rather than simply replace them. Therefore, it is about understanding how AI could affect the areas we want to work in (i.e. that align with our interests and needs/values) and plan our skill development accordingly.

As author and futurist Bernard Marr writes:

"Rather than succumb to the doomsday predictions that 'robots will take over all the jobs', a more optimistic outlook is one where humans get the opportunity to do work that demands their creativity, imagination, social and emotional intelligence, and passion. Individuals will need to act and engage in lifelong learning, so they are adaptable when the changes happen ... Employees will need to shape their own career path. Gone are the days when a career trajectory is outlined at one company with predictable climbs up the corporate ladder. Therefore, employees should take the initiative to shape their own career paths. Individuals will need to step into the opportunity that pursuing your passion provides rather than shrink back to what had resulted in success in the past. This shift in work opens the possibility to achieve more of our potential."[21]

This is the whole reason I have written this book: to give you the skills to manage your own career and find and keep your career sweet spot – in other words, so you have career agility in this everchanging work landscape.

In terms of the second force that Deloitte has identified, this is really about what a lot of people are calling the gig economy. The *Oxford Dictionary* defines the gig economy as "a labour market characterized by the prevalence of short-term contracts or freelance work as opposed to permanent jobs".

As the reliance on permanent employees decreases and the use of contractors and consultants increases, this will suit some people in terms of their personal preferences and lifestyle needs more than others. While I really enjoy flexibility because I have a primary-school-aged daughter, my personal preference is to be part of a permanent team. I have a strong preference for extroversion (using the Myers–Briggs definition) and a strong preference for structure (again using Myers–Briggs) so I have found a way to be a consultant/contractor but also put some structure around my working arrangement. Through trial and error, and communication with my employer, we have found an arrangement that works for us both. It took me a while, but I have found an arrangement that works for me and works in the job market.

While permanent employment opportunities are decreasing, several options remain. These include a portfolio career, which as leadership specialist Michael Greenspan puts it, is "a curated and interesting medley of part-time roles".[22] There is self-employment, job sharing – the list goes on. Many of these ways of working were not options in my parents' generation. I combine my own business and sub-contracting to several larger companies, which is what works best for me at the moment. I encourage you to talk to lots of people in your network and explore all the different options and ways of working out there to find the one that best works for you.

The future of work and emerging occupations

I also encourage you to keep up to date with the skills that are required in the job market and those that will be needed in the future. Many reputable organisations publish regular reports with this kind of valuable information, including the World Economic Forum, Organisation for Economic Co-operation and Development (OECD) and the online professional network LinkedIn.

In August 2020, the Australian National Skills Commission released a list of 25 emerging occupations offering valuable insights into future opportunities for job seekers and students. The full list can be viewed on its website.[23] In 2018, the World Economic Forum published *The Future of Jobs Report*.[24] It looks at the trends expected in the period 2018 to 2022 in 20 economies and 12 industry sectors. In summary, it outlines five key findings:[25]

1. Automation, robotisation and digitisation look different across different industries.
2. There is a net positive outlook for jobs – amid significant job disruption.
3. The division of labour between humans, machines and algorithms is shifting fast.
4. New tasks at work are driving demand for new skills.
5. We will all need to become lifelong learners.

If these key findings are true, then being agile in your career management can only help you in negotiating your way through these changes.

The OECD has also published some great information about the future of work. According to its analysis, advances in technology are unlikely to lead to fewer jobs for humans. "While technological progress makes some occupations obsolete, it also creates new jobs."[26]

So, it is about understanding what these new jobs will be and how well they align to your skills, interests and values – essentially being career agile. The best way to find out about this is to continue to research and find out what is happening in the job market, reading and talking to people.

When researching/networking and talking to people most career coaches recommend you use the A.I.R. approach, which is asking for advice, information or insights and referrals.

When talking to people, you might like to ask them some of the following questions:

- Given your skills, interests, and needs (which you will now be able to professionally and succinctly articulate) what jobs/companies/industries do they think would suit you?
- Given your skills, interest and needs, what jobs/companies/industries would you be able to add value to?
- If they know you well from a work perspective, do they agree with your list of skills and your self-rating in terms of proficiency level from exercise 5?
- If you have a particular target in mind, are there any skills that they think you need to further develop? Again, use the information from exercise 5.
- What trends are they seeing in the job market?
- If you have a particular industry in mind or if they have suggested you consider a particular industry, what trends are they seeing in the industry you want to move into?
- If you have a particular job target in mind, what is the 'day in the life' like for someone in that job?
- If you have a particular job target in mind and they do this job, what do they like about their job? What do they dislike about their job?

- What other research would they recommend you do?
- Is there anyone else they would recommend you speak to?
- Is there anyone in their network that could help you with your research that they would be happy to introduce you to?

Exercise twenty-one

The above questions are just thought starters. Write down below or in your notebook any areas you would like to learn more about and any questions you would like to ask as part of your research.

_____
_____
_____
_____
_____
_____
_____
_____

VERONICA MILLEN

10

Bringing it all together

Congratulations on getting this far! Now let's bring together all of your hard work and all of the thinking you have done so far.

Start by transcribing your 'top 5' answers from the ends of chapters 6, 7 and 8 and reflections from Chapter 9 into the diagram on the next page.

Then I encourage you to spend some time reflecting on what job or career or industry is (or could be) at the intersection of the elements. For some of you this may be obvious; for others this may be more of a challenge.

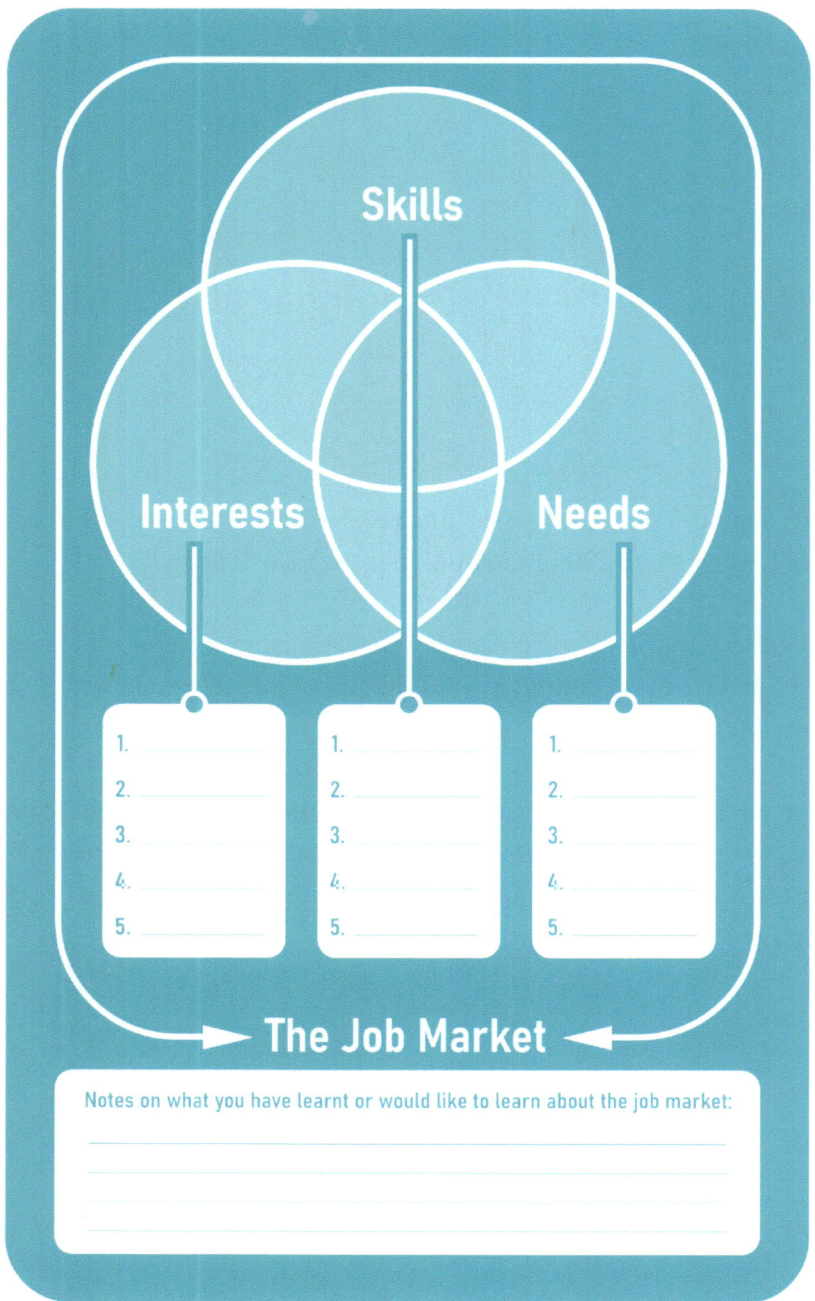

Meeting all four areas (skills, interests, needs and the job market)

It is important to try and ensure that all four areas are met at least to some degree.

- If you don't have the skills required, it may prove difficult to land a job in this area. So, you will need to think about what you are willing to do to gain the skills, for example through further studies or an internship. Are you willing to invest the time and money needed to build the skill or skills required? Some career coaches call this a 'reality check'. Are you really willing to do what it takes to move into a new career? The time required will depend on what level of skill you need and/or want to develop. In his book *Outliers: The Story of Success*, Malcolm Gladwell quotes neurologist Daniel Levitin and studies that show that it takes 10,000 hours of practice to achieve the level of mastery associated with being a world-class expert – in anything.[27]
- If you don't have the interest in the role or career, ultimately, I think you will be unfulfilled, dissatisfied and unhappy.
- If your personal work needs are not met, it will be hard to sustain this situation long term as none of us are truly fulfilled when our key needs/values are not met.
- If there is something that fulfils all three elements (skills, interests and needs) of the model but there is no job market, you will need to think about how you may be able to monetise what you do. There are some great resources available to support people in doing this. For example Laura Clarke's article entitled 'How to Monetize Your Passion'.[28]

This is why I believe that finding a role or career that meets all elements will be the most rewarding and sustainable position for each of us.

You may find that your needs are met to a greater extent in one area than another, for example you may choose to sacrifice some income for greater interest in your work, but it is important that all of the four areas are met to a base level. For some people, all four areas are met to a high degree and this is the ideal.

Uncovering your strengths

Uncovering your 'strengths' may help you bring together your skills, interests and needs. Strengths can be defined from a positive psychology perspective as things you are good at, and like doing.

Traditionally, psychology focused on 'deficits' such as anxiety, depression, bi-polar and other mental illnesses and the treatment of these, which is a noble cause. It wasn't until the early 2000s – relatively recent in scientific research terms – that some scientists came together to study character strengths rather than deficits. From a Human Resources point of view, this was exciting as asking people to focus on building their strengths is far more intuitive and likely to be successful than asking people to improve on something that they are not good at or don't like doing.

While at work we need to meet minimum standards. Once our skills meet these standards, we can flourish by focusing on building our strengths. This approach has turned development planning on its head. Rather than asking employees to pick something they are weak at, and look at ways to improve in that area, Human Resources professionals started (and encouraged managers to start) identifying strengths and looking at how they could be built on. Like everything in life, balance is important and any strength to the extreme can be a weakness, so it is important for us all to identify if we are ever over-playing a certain strength.

Some of the researchers who came together to study strengths identified 24 character strengths that apply across cultures. In 2004, Christopher Peterson and Martin Seligman published the VIA (Values In Action) Classification of Character Strengths and Virtues. This is a classification of positive traits in human beings and outlines the 24 VIA character strengths in detail. The researchers identified that every individual possesses all of the 24 character strengths but in different degrees, thereby giving each person a unique character profile.

The exciting thing about character strengths is that research shows that people who use their character strengths every day are three times more likely to report having an excellent quality of life and six times more likely to be engaged at work.[29] This shows the importance of knowing your strengths and using them at work. This is why I encourage you to identify your skills, interests and needs, because together they form your strengths. Knowing and being able to articulate your strengths will help you to move towards your career sweet spot.

If you would like to find out more about character strengths and your unique character profile, you may like to undertake the free VIA character strengths survey. A link to the survey is provided on my website at **www.veronicamillen.com/career-agility**.

Research shows that using your character strengths can help you at work, but also:

- improve your relationships;
- enhance health and overall wellbeing; and
- buffer against, manage and overcome problems.[30]

So, there are many benefits to exploring your character strengths.

I think it is important to do the detailed work I have outlined in the earlier exercises in this book before going straight to the VIA strengths questionnaire, as I believe you will get value from this granular reflection in terms of understanding your specific skills, interests and needs. This detailed understanding will be important criteria when researching roles, companies and industries that will suit you. Doing the VIA strengths questionnaire is a great way to add more depth to your self-discovery journey and the additional information and insights from the survey may support you in finding your career sweet spot.

Exercise twenty-two

If you complete the VIA character strengths survey, write down below or in your notebook anything you learn about your strengths and any thoughts you have about how this inputs into your career sweet spot.

_____
_____
_____
_____
_____
_____
_____
_____

For example:

According to the VIA survey, my top character strength is love. At first when I read this result, I was a bit surprised and confused, especially because I was thinking about my work and career. But as I researched and learnt more about character strengths and the character strength of love, it began to make more sense to me. I began to learn that the VIA Institute sees love as a strength within the virtue category of humanity, one of six virtues that subcategorise the 24 strengths. Humanity describes strengths that manifest in caring relationships with others. These strengths are interpersonal and are mostly relevant in one-on-one relationships. The other strengths in humanity are kindness, love and social intelligence. When I reflect on what I am good at and like doing, it often involves building strong relationships, and when I think about the feedback I receive, it is often about my social intelligence and ability to build and maintain strong relationships – both in and out of work.

A note on confidence and self-compassion

Many of us have times when our confidence waivers. The term 'imposter syndrome' exists for a reason. You may not have imposter syndrome, but your confidence may be holding you back from moving towards your career sweet spot.

If this is the case, firstly, this is very normal. American talk show host Oprah Winfrey says that every person she has ever interviewed – including the former President of the United States Barack Obama and singer Beyoncé – has asked her the same question: "After every interview, at some point somebody would say, 'How was that? Was that OK? How'd I do?'" These questions, she says, are the "common denominator" for all her guests, no matter who they are.[31]

Secondly, only 50 percent of confidence is genetic. Self-confidence can be expanded through deliberate choice.[32] If you are interested in learning more about this, I highly recommend two books: *The Confidence Code* by Katty Kay and Claire Shipman (published by HarperCollins) and *The Power of Real Confidence* by Michelle Sales (published by Major Street). Megan Dalla-Camina also does amazing work in this space and has a free online guide (www.megandallacamina.com/confidenceguide). So, if confidence is holding you back from moving towards your dream job, please consider doing some work in this area as I believe you will see some positive results.

Linked to confidence is the concept of self-compassion, which is very different to self-pity. Dr Kristin Neff is a pioneer researcher on the topic of self-compassion. She has identified three key elements of self-compassion: self-kindness, common humanity and mindfulness. Self-compassion entails being warm and understanding towards ourselves when we suffer, fail or feel inadequate. According to her research, self-compassion is on the opposite spectrum of self-criticism.

Self-compassion allows and inspires us to learn from failures and to try again. Self-criticism, on the other hand, might lead to giving up or denying our failures.[33]

I am sure you can see the importance of self-compassion as you are on your self-discovery and career journey, and how it will help you to keep going. One of the elements that I find particularly useful from Neff's work on self-compassion is the idea of talking to yourself as you would your best friend. If you think you may need to cultivate your self-compassion, I highly recommend Neff's book *Self-Compassion: The Proven Power of Being Kind to Yourself* (published by William Morrow and Company).

Researching

Talking to a lot of people may help you find jobs and industries that meet all career agility elements for you. Once you know your key skills, interests and values, you can have articulate conversations with people to uncover whether the jobs/careers/industries they work in align with your career sweet spot. The more you read and talk to people, the more you will learn and the closer you will be to finding your ideal role or career.

When people ask you what you are looking for or what you want to do, you may not have a one-word answer like 'accounting', but you will be able to outline your skills, interests and needs. They will then understand what you are looking for and what value you may add. They will then be able to advise you on what would suit your unique combination of skills, interests and needs. If they don't offer this information, I would encourage you to ask. People usually like to help others and offer advice. Ask people what role/careers/industries they think would best suit you. You may learn a lot from their answers. You may not always agree, but you will have the information to make an informed decision.

If you are approached about a role or if you see a role advertised, I recommend that you critically review the role against your criteria, i.e. do you have the required skills or can you (and are you willing to) build those skills? Is it aligned with your interests? Does it meet your personal needs or work values? If you don't have the data to answer any of these questions, do some research to find out the information through the interview and selection process.

For example:

When I was working as an in-house coach for a large corporate, an employee considered to have high potential was referred to me for coaching. Her primary objective was to determine what she wanted to do next in her career as she wasn't enjoying her current role and wanted to move into something she would enjoy.

Through our coaching sessions, she completed her 'archaeological dig'. When I first spoke to her about this exercise, she had thought there were no common threads through her work history. To her credit, she took the time and completed the exercises I suggested. From doing some deep reflection, talking to her husband about what she used to complain or speak positively about after work, and through our coaching sessions, she uncovered that there were some trends after all. She really liked being part of a team, being responsible for a piece of work from beginning to end, and autonomy. She also loved making things smoother and hadn't known this was called process improvement or process re-design – a transferrable and desirable skill.

As we worked together, she became clearer and was able to articulate to her mentor and the Human Resources team what she wanted to do next. By uncovering her skills and preferences, she was able to explain that she was open in terms of her next role (it didn't have to have a particular title) but was looking for an opportunity where she could deliver process improvements and be a strong team player. She was successful in gaining another role internally that aligned well with her personal attributes. I loved bumping into her in the tearoom from time to time and seeing how happy she was in her new role. This was thanks to her work reflecting and researching roles that would align with her skills, interests and needs.

It is also interesting to note that about two years after she had started in this role, I ran into her again and asked how she was going. This time she said she was no longer enjoying the job; her new manager had a different leadership style and had changed some of the aspects of her job. However, she went on to say that while she was unhappy, she now had the skills and tools to know what to do and how to manage the situation. Only the night before she had pulled out the folder from our coaching sessions and was revisiting what we had discussed. I like to think that I gave her some strong career agility skills that she can use for life, and that this book can do the same for you.

CAREER AGILITY

Your overall reflections and action plan

Exercise twenty-three

What are your reflections from all the exercises? Review all your answers in relation to your skills, interests and needs. Look for patterns. Are there any consistent themes? Does anything jump out to you? Write down below or in your notebook any additional thoughts you have now that you have reviewed all your answers.

_____
_____
_____
_____
_____
_____
_____
_____

Exercise twenty-four

What ideas do you have now about your ideal job career sweet spot? Write down below or in your notebook any ideas you have based on all the thinking you have done and how it all comes together.

_____
_____
_____
_____
_____
_____
_____
_____

Exercise twenty-five

What actions are you going to take now?

This exercise is really important. Research shows that writing down goals and actions and tracking progress is highly correlated with achievement. For example, one study showed that 76 percent of participants who wrote down their goals and actions, and provided weekly progress to a friend, successfully achieved their goals. This result was 33 percent higher than those participants with unwritten goals, with a success rate of only 43 percent of goals achieved. This study shows the value of taking the time to write down your goals, create an action plan and develop a system of support to hold yourself accountable for achieving your goals.[34] Therefore, I highly recommend you write down your goals and actions and track them.

One of my favourite quotes, and one I often have to remind myself of, is "Do or not do. There is no try" (Yoda – *Star Wars*). For me, this really sums up the importance of action.

You may like to use the template provided in this book or write your own action plan in your notebook, but we know that moving forward in our career takes action.

Goal	Action required	Barriers

Resources	Additional considerations	Due date for action

I recommend you undertake this analysis every few years as your personal circumstances may change and also the world of work is changing so quickly that even if your requirements haven't changed, there may be new jobs and industries that better align to your career sweet spot.

Regular reflection of your skills, interests and needs and action (adjustment if necessary) to ensure this aligns with your work is true career agility and I believe can enable a fulfilling and sustainable career. To help you along, perhaps consider teaming up with a 'career buddy' so you can support each other and keep each other accountable through your career journeys.

Don't worry if you are still not 100 percent clear on what your ideal job is. For some people, this is a longer process and can take more time. You may need to continue the process and reflect further and continue your career discussions. You should at least be closer to understanding the elements that comprise your dream role or ideal career. If you are still struggling, you might like to contact a career coach to support you.

While you are working on uncovering your skills, interests, and needs and understanding the job market you may like to consider job crafting. Job crafting is changing your job to make it more engaging and meaningful[35]. Job crafting takes three main forms. The first is task crafting, which involves altering the type, scope, sequence and number of tasks that make up your job. The second is relational crafting where you craft your job by altering those you interact with in your work. Thirdly there is cognitive crafting where you modify the way you interpret the tasks and/or work you're doing. If you want to know more about job crafting there is a lot of information available online so doing a simple and quick google search is a good place to start.

The next and final chapter features real life journeys with people who are now working in their career sweet spot. This wasn't always the case for them; they made some changes and in doing so aligned their work with their skills, interests and needs. Each person has taken a different journey but all are now fulfilled in their work. So, please read on. I hope you are as inspired by their stories as I am.

11

Bringing it to life

This chapter contains some real-life examples of people I know whose work is well aligned to their skills, interests and values. They are paid to do work they love. Sure, they may have bad days, but overall, they are in their career sweet spot. This has not always been the case for them, and it is worthwhile reading about real life journeys and how people have achieved career fulfilment.

In talking to these people, they didn't knowingly use or apply the career agility model (or any career management model), but when they reflect on why they are happy in their jobs and careers they all agree that all elements of the model are met for them and that is why they are satisfied. They feel they have the skills for their work and that it aligns well with their interests and needs/values. There is also a market for their work so that this is now their full-time job and not just a hobby.

Colin Beattie

Colin and I worked together at National Australia Bank in Human Resources from 1998 to 2002. Colin studied economics and accounting at university and started his career in a chartered accounting firm. He now runs a successful consulting business and is the Founder of The People Spot. Colin works within organisations to unleash people's potential, teams' potential, and even the potential of the organisation itself – and he loves it! He has been consulting and coaching for almost 20 years now, and also produces a fantastic podcast called 'Leadership of Fools'.

When I spoke with Colin about his career, he said he studied economics and accounting at university because he wasn't aware of all the options and this was something that others were also going to study, and it was a fun time socially. He enjoyed his time in his first corporate job at a chartered accounting firm because it met some of his needs such as being part of a group, but he didn't love and wasn't necessarily naturally skilled at the accounting work itself. When he helped to train some of the new accountants, he found that work really satisfying, so he pursued this as he realised it was something he was good at and enjoyed. He also began to realise that he valued autonomy and choice and freedom, which fit well with consulting.

Over the past 18 years, Colin has done work that he enjoys and is good at, and has carved out a market niche that is based on his skill set. Given he really enjoys what he does, his skills continue to grow as he is happy to spend time learning more and further developing his craft.

Natalie Wheeler and Kristy Sadler

I have known Natalie since 2007. At the time, she was working at Goldman Sachs J B Were. When she had her daughter in 2011, she met and became close friends with Kristy through a local mothers' group. They discovered they both loved Scandinavian design, and that it was difficult to buy beautiful Scandinavian-designed products in Australia. In late 2013 after a lot of hard work, website development and product sourcing, they launched an online store and a year later opened their first bricks and mortar retail store.

Nat and Kristy were strategic and started with an online shop to test the market while they had returned to their corporate roles post parental leave. This meant that they didn't have huge start-up costs like rent and they had a fallback plan if it didn't work out; it also helped them fund the growth of the business in the early stages.

Fast forward to today, and Natalie and Kristy have both left the corporate world and love running Norsu, an incredibly successful retail company that has featured on the 'The Block' renovation television show and has more than 335,000 followers on Instagram. What I love about their journey is that they combine the elements of career agility: they love interiors, they are both good at design, and there is a market for the beautiful homewares they sell and the design services they provide.

While they work long hours, they love what they do and it aligns with their values in terms of balancing work and family. During the COVID-19 pandemic, they have successfully pivoted to offer online design consultations and other services. I am really inspired by their journey and their career agility.

Rick Fontyn

I have known Rick since 2005. Rick started his career in banking, and then went on to work in financial services for more than a decade. His passion has always been for sport and his home state of Tasmania.

Combining this passion with his skills in public speaking and presenting, Rick has gone on to become a successful sports commentator, producer and host. He now works as an announcer for the Brisbane Tennis International, is a ground announcer for the Hawthorn AFL Football Club and hosts an online sports program called 'Talking Sport Tasmania'.

Rick is also the producer and host of 'Make it in Tasmania' which successfully launched in November 2020.

Rick and his family live in Tasmania, so by focusing on sport and local business in his home state he has been able to combine his love of sport and Tasmania and skills in presenting with what he values, which is spending time with his family.

Rick's determination to work hard to have a career that he enjoys and is good at is really inspiring.

Jonathan Millen

I met my husband Jonathan in 2005 when we were both working in Human Resources (HR) at National Australia Bank. Before moving into HR, Jono had spent over a decade in banking, mainly in business banking. It was an area he has 'fallen into' and wasn't enjoying. He moved into the training team in HR at National Australia Bank because a friend and former colleague from business banking encouraged him to make the change. It wasn't based on a detailed analysis of his skills and interests, but luckily he enjoyed the work and had great underlying potential for this type of work.

Before I met him Jono had completed a Diploma in Finance and he often told me he didn't want to study again as he hadn't enjoyed the experience. Once he found work he enjoyed he was happy to study again and build his skills in that area. He has now completed two post-graduate qualifications focusing on leadership and coaching. Whilst these studies were challenging he enjoyed learning and building his skills because the courses aligned with his interests.

Jono is now an accomplished people leader with consistently high engagement scores for the teams he leads. He receives fantastic feedback from the sessions he facilitates. He is recognised as a Professional Certified Coach (PCC) by the International Coaching Federation (ICF). I love reading the feedback from the people who have been in his team or attended one of his workshops or he has coached one on one. They all rave about the positive impact he has had on their lives.

One of the reasons I wanted to share Jono's career is because it demonstrates that you don't always have to move out of corporate work to be happy, which seems to be a common misconception. Also if you haven't enjoyed study in the past you may find you enjoy it if it is aligned to your area(s) of interest.

With all of these examples the individuals have pivoted and shown great career agility (albeit inadvertently) to better align their skills, interests and values with the job market, which has resulted in greater career satisfactions.

I hope that by reading about their careers you have been inspired and can see how the career agility model can be applied to real life journeys – including yours.

12

A note about COVID-19

The majority of this book was written before the Coronavirus global pandemic. At first, I thought I should shelve the book as lots of people have been made redundant and lost their jobs and cannot afford to be picky about their next job. But then I was talking to a friend and former colleague who said that maybe right now career agility is more important than ever. Maybe we all need to find ways to think more broadly about our skills, for example, and how transferrable they are. So, if your job has been impacted by the pandemic, I hope that this book can help you think about your career agility, in particular your transferrable skills, and researching the job market – ultimately to find work that you are good at and enjoy.

13

Endnotes

1. S Denning, *The Age of Agile, How Smart Companies Are Transforming the Way Work Gets Done*, AMACON, 2018.
2. *ibid.*
3. *ibid.*
4. C Myers, 'How to Find your Ikigai And Transform Your Outlook On Life and Business', *Forbes*, 23 February 2018, viewed 16 October 2020, <https://www.forbes.com/sites/chrismyers/2018/02/23/how-to-find-your-ikigai-and-transform-your-outlook-on-life-and-business/#5ba33fc52ed4>.
5. Gettysburg College, 'One third of your life is spent at work', Gettysburg College, 2020, viewed 26 October 2020, <http://www.gettysburg.edu/news_events/press_release_detail.dot?id=79db7b34-630c-4f49-ad32-4ab9ea48e72b>.
6. H Whelan, *Charting and finding your fulfilling career*, Success television, n.d., viewed 16 October 2020, <https://successtelevision.com/index.php/Career/charting-and-finding-your-fulfilling-career.html>.
7. M Csikszentmihalyi, 'Flow, the secret to happiness', TED2004, TED, February 2004, viewed 19 October

2020, <https://www.ted.com/talks/mihaly_csikszentmihalyi_flow_the_secret_to_happiness?language=en>.

8. M Oppland, '8 Ways To Create Flow According to Mihaly Csikszentmihalyi', positivepsychology.com, n.d., viewed 19 October 2020, <https://positivepsychology.com/mihaly-csikszentmihalyi-father-of-flow/>.

9. D Bortz, 'Your work values can help you find the right job', Monster, n.d., viewed 19 October 2020, <https://www.monster.com/career-advice/article/work-values-check-list>.

10. J Maxwell, 'Do You Get the Five Benefits of Work?', joannamaxwell.com.au, 15 March 2016, viewed 19 October 2020, <https://www.joannamaxwell.com.au/do-you-get-the-five-benefits-of-work/>.

11. J De Neve & G Ward, 'Does Work Make You Happy? Evidence from the World Happiness Report', *Harvard Business Review*, 20 March 2017, viewed 19 October 2020, <https://hbr.org/2017/03/does-work-make-you-happy-evidence-from-the-world-happiness-report>.

12. P Docker, D Mead & S Sinek, *Find Your Why: A Practical Guide for Discovering Purpose for You and Your Team*, Penguin UK, 2017, pp. 6–7.

13. P Docker, D Mead & S Sinek, *Find Your Why: A Practical Guide for Discovering Purpose for You and Your Team*, Penguin UK, 2017, p. 54.

14. J Maxwell, *Rethink your career in your 40s, 50s and 60s*, ABC Books, 2018, p. 100.

15. See www.megandallacamina.com

16. See www.lorrainemurphy.com.au

17. See www.instagram.com/jackdelosa and www.the-entourage.com/jack-delosa

18. C Taylor, 'The Nomad Economy', Korn Ferry, viewed on 3rd July 2021, <https://www.kornferry.com/content/

19. L Walsh, 'The future of work: 17 jobs and five different careers', The Sydney Morning Herald, 28 July 2016, viewed on 3rd July 2021, <https://www.smh.com.au/opinion/the-future-of-work-17-jobs-and-five-different-careers-20170728-gxko39.html>
20. Deloitte Insights, 'Future of Work', Deloitte, 2020, viewed 20 October 2020, <https://www2.deloitte.com/us/en/insights/focus/technology-and-the-future-of-work.html>.
21. B Marr, 'The Future of Work: 5 Important Ways Jobs Will Change in the 4th Industrial Revolution', *Forbes*, 15 July 2019, viewed 20 October 2020, <https://www.forbes.com/sites/bernardmarr/2019/07/15/the-future-of-work-5-important-ways-jobs-will-change-in-the-4th-industrial-revolution/#7b8cc06b54c7>.
22. M Greenspan, 'How to Launch a Successful Portfolio Career', *Harvard Business Review*, 4 May 2017, <https://hbr.org/2017/05/how-to-launch-a-successful-portfolio-career>.
23. National Skills Commission, 'Emerging occupations', National Skills Commission, Australian Government, n.d., viewed 20 October 2020, <https://www.nationalskillscommission.gov.au/emerging-occupations>.
24. World Economic Forum, *The Future of Jobs Report 2018*, Centre for the New Economy and Society, World Economic Forum, Geneva, 2018, viewed 20 October 2020, <http://www3.weforum.org/docs/WEF_Future_of_Jobs_2018.pdf>.
25. TA Leopold & V Ratcheva, '5 things to know about the future of jobs', World Economic Forum, 17 September

2018, viewed 20 October 2020, <https://www.weforum.org/agenda/2018/09/future-of-jobs-2018-things-to-know>.
26. OECD, 'Data on the Future of work,' OECD, n.d., viewed 20 October 2020, <https://www.oecd.org/els/emp/future-of-work/data/>.
27. M Gladwell, *Outliers: The Story of Success*, Little, Brown and Company, United States, 2011, p. 40.
28. L Clarke, 'How to Monetize Your Passion', *Lifehack*, n.d., viewed 5 November 2020, <https://www.lifehack.org/articles/money/how-monetize-your-passion.html>.
29. VIA Institute on Character, 'Character strengths', VIA Institute on Character, 2020, n.d., viewed 19 October 2020, <https://www.viacharacter.org/character-strengths-via>.
30. *ibid*.
31. J Nededog, 'Oprah says every guest asks her the same question after their interviews – but she was still shocked when Beyoncé asked it', *Insider*, 24 September 2017, viewed 5 November 2020, <https://www.insider.com/oprah-winfrey-question-every-guests-asks-after-interviews-beyonce-2017-9>.
32. M Selig, 'No Confidence? No Problem. Use These 7 Strategies Instead', *Psychology Today*, 11 July 2018, viewed 5 November 2030, <https://www.psychologytoday.com/us/blog/changepower/201807/no-confidence-no-problem-use-these-7-strategies-instead>.
33. The Pavlovic Today, 'Self-compassion: Treat Yourself Like a Best Friend', *The Pavlovic Today*, 4 December 2016, viewed 5 November 2020, <https://www.thepavlovictoday.com/inspiration/self-compassion/>.
34. J Traugott, 'Achieving your goals: An evidence-based approach', Michigan State University, 26 August 2014,

viewed 5 November 2020,<https://www.canr.msu.edu/news/achieving_your_goals_an_evidence_based_approach>.

35. J Dutton & A Wresniewski, 'What Job Crafting Looks Like', *Harvard Business Review*, 12 March 2020, viewed 28 June 2021, <https://hbr.org/2020/03/what-job-crafting-looks-like>.

VERONICA MILLEN

14

Thank you

"You can't be what you can't see." – Marian Wright Edelman

Thank you to my parents who role-modelled hard work for me. They came to Australia 50 years ago and had very little. They worked very hard to make a wonderful life for my sister and me. I will always be grateful for their love and support. I endeavour to work hard based on the wonderful example they set for me.

Thank you to my husband Jonathan. His dedication to ongoing learning and applying what he has learnt is truly inspiring. He really does try to be the best he can be and has always encouraged and supported me.

Thank you to my daughter Eleanor who inspires me to be a positive role model.

Thank you to my sister Natasha who is the best sister and cheerleader a girl could ask for.

Thank you to my friends. Those who let me feature their journeys in this book. Those who encouraged me as I wrote this book. Those who have supported me in my career and in my personal life.

Thank you to Ellen Jackson, a good friend of mine since 1990 when we started our undergraduate studies together, who wrote the foreword for this book.

Thank you to Melanie Scaife, a good friend of mine from primary school, who did a fantastic job of editing this book.

Thank you to Alan Macfarlane. His input and advice in relation to graphics is greatly appreciated.

A special thank you to Nerissa Beattie. Nerissa and I used to work together at National Australia Bank in the 1990s and early 2000s; I reported to her and she was a great leader. We have remained friends and love catching up, talking about anything from family to coaching and everything in between. I admire Nerissa greatly. She is a psychologist and moved from the world of organisational psychology to working as a psychologist in schools. She is a great example of doing meaningful work that she is good at, enjoys and aligns with her values around helping others, in particular youth. Nerissa gave me the great idea for the title of this book. Thanks Nerissa!

15

About the author

Veronica Millen is a senior Human Resource professional with more than 20 years' experience working for large ASX-listed organisations across a wide range of industries, including energy, property, retail, and financial services. During this time, she has gained expertise in organisational development, talent identification and development, diversity and inclusion, employee experience and organisational culture.

Veronica has also run her own consulting firm for over a decade, providing specialised coaching and consulting services to a range of clients including large corporates, small businesses, government departments and individual private clients. Some of Veronica's clients have included MYOB, BHP, Aprelo, Somersault Consulting, Grace Papers, PowerPlant, Let's Talk Career, David Challis International, The Climate Change Authority and The Victorian SES.

Veronica holds a Bachelor of Economics and Commerce from Melbourne University and has completed post graduate studies in Leadership and Management. Veronica also holds a certificate IV in Workplace and Business Coaching; and a Diploma in Workplace and Business Coaching.

Veronica is committed to her ongoing development and building her skills so she can better support her clients; for example Veronica has completed short courses in The Science of Wellbeing (Yale University via Coursera) and Positive Psychology (The University of North Carolina at Chapel Hill via Coursera).

Veronica is accredited in the Birkman Method, the Morrisby career profile, the Myers Briggs Type Indicator (MBTI), the Life Styles Inventory (LSI) & the Group Styles Inventory (GSI), the Emotional and Social Competence Inventory (ESCI - Korn Ferry), using VIA character Strengths at work; and Mental Health First Aid.

Veronica is a passionate career coach and a member of the Career Development Association of Australia (CDAA).

Veronica has over 800 hours of coaching experience and has been accredited as a Professional Certified Coach (PCC) by the International Coaching Federation (ICF).

Veronica is passionate and skilled at working with people one on one or in groups via facilitation to bring out their best, supporting people to identify and articulate their strengths.

For more information visit **www.veronicamillen.com**.

16

Notes

This notes section provides space for you to write any notes, thoughts or reflections you have while reading this book.

VERONICA MILLEN

CAREER AGILITY

VERONICA MILLEN

VERONICA MILLEN

VERONICA MILLEN

www.ingramcontent.com/pod-product-compliance
Lightning Source LLC
Chambersburg PA
CBHW041500010526
44107CB00044B/1510